GEOGRAPHY ENCYCLOPEDIA

UNDERSTANDING NATURE AND WORKING WITH IT

Om Books International

Contents

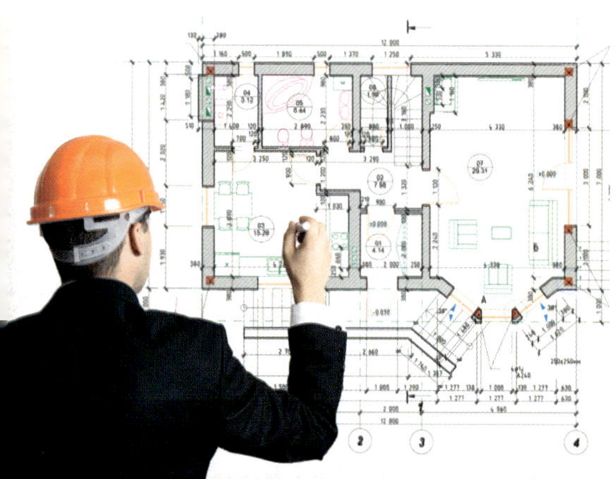

NATURE'S DISASTERS

There are certain phenomena in nature that produce hazardous effects. These hazards are deadly and destructive. They take lives and destroy property. Some change the shape of a landscape forever. Some disasters last for a few minutes, but to repair the destruction that they leave behind takes years.

We cannot prevent a natural disaster from taking place. However, we can keep ourselves alert and on watch for them. Studies have been made to predict and estimate when these disasters will strike next. During a natural disaster, we can act fast and keep ourselves safe.

LIGHTNING, THUNDERSTORMS AND TORNADOES

Have you ever seen lightning in the sky? It is a current of light which starts at the clouds and travels to the ground. It can even travel from the ground to the clouds or from cloud to cloud. A thunder is a loud booming sound heard just after a lightning. It is caused by the sudden expansion of air in the path of an electrical discharge. Lightning and thunder are features of a thunderstorm.

Recipe for a thunderstorm

To form a thunderstorm, there must be moisture in the air, there must be unstable air rising upwards and there must be something to cause the air to rise upwards. Unstable air is a type of air that rises upwards with a simple nudge. In the case of thunderstorms, this nudge is provided by heat.

Rising air

During the day, the ground gets heated by the hot rays of the Sun. The air closer to the ground also heats up and rises up. The cool air from above sinks towards the Earth. The warm air will continue to rise if it is warmer (which means lighter) than the surrounding air. This air will transfer some of its heat to the surrounding atmosphere, especially the upper layers. The rising air, starts to cool and begins to lose some of the water vapour. It slowly condenses and forms a cloud, which then moves upwards to a part of the atmosphere which experiences below freezing temperatures.

Formation of a thunderstorm

When these clouds come into contact with unstable air and are forced up a mountain or hill, they cause orographic thunderstorms. When these clouds come across the borders of a weather front, they cause frontal thunderstorms. When the unstable air mass experiences convection, it causes air mass thunderstorms.

FUN FACT

THUNDERSTORM

Tornadoes are also called "twisters" or "cyclones". They have been witnessed in all continents except Antarctica. A tornado is measured using a Fujita scale, where F0 stands for minimum damage, while F5 indicates heavy damage.

Anvils

A thunderstorm looks like the flowery head of a cauliflower. It has a cloud formation that occurs in the upper portion of the storm. This formation is called the "anvil". When the warm air rises, which is called an updraft, it reaches a point where the air around is even warmer than it is. At this point, the cloud stops moving and flattens in the shape of an anvil. Anvil clouds are mostly made up of icy particles. The shape that they form looks a lot like an anvil, which gives this formation its name.

An approaching anvil thunderstorm.

A representation of the supercell tornado over the Great Plains.

An approaching tornado.

Calculating the distance

We can understand how far away a thunderstorm is from us by counting the time between a lightning bolt and thunder. This time should then be divided by five to understand the approximate distance in kilometres. If we hear a thunder 15 seconds after we see a lightning bolt, then the thunderstorm is roughly 3–4 km away.

Lightning

During a thunderstorm, we first see a lightning and then hear thunder. This is because light travels faster than sound. A lightning is a massive spark of electricity. It can spread to a distance of 8 km. A single spark of lightning is called a bolt of lightning. One bolt of lightning can power the batteries of 80 million cars.

Tornado

Like a thunderstorm, a tornado is a storm which sees winds speedily rotating. It looks like a funnel-shaped column. This tornado starts from a cloud and reaches down to the ground. The winds blow powerfully when closer to the ground. They move from their original position and, depending upon their power, might cover a distance of 500 km, causing destruction along the way.

How does a tornado form?

The formation of a tornado is not yet completely understood. A rotating thunderstorm is called a supercell. A tornado starts from this supercell. Scientists are still struggling with understanding its formation. It is difficult to get an equipment into a tornado or get close enough to study it. A tornado destroys everything in its path.

Strength of a tornado

Tornadoes are very sudden. They can begin at any time. A moving tornado is so strong that it can thrash a house and uproot trees. A light object can be carried almost 3,000 m into the air. It stars from a supercell.

A tornado can last for a few seconds or ten minutes. Within this time, they can change a landscape beyond recognition.

HURRICANES

A hurricane is another type of storm. It is also called a tropical cyclone. It takes place over tropical or subtropical bodies of water. They are massive storms that can move with a wind speed of 257 kmph. A hurricane can unleash 9 trillion litres of rain in one day.

Formation of a hurricane

The winds unleashed by a hurricane move so fast that they can destroy the buildings in their path. They can uproot trees and lift up cars on the way. So, where do hurricanes form? They form over warm ocean water (this is why they take place in tropical or subtropical areas). The swirling water sometimes hits the land with great force. Hurricanes cause storms on land and also heavy rains which give rise to heavy floods.

In 1945, the coastline of Florida was flooded due to a hurricane travelling from the Bahamas to the east coast. The waters travelled for seven days with great force.

From a storm to a hurricane

The first stage of a hurricane is a storm. This storm forms from a disturbance in the tropical waters. Specifically, a storm starts over a warm area of the ocean over which rain clouds are just forming. This area is called an area of "tropical disturbance".

Sometimes, a tropical disturbance moves into an area of "tropical depression" where there are rotating thunderstorms with winds that move at a speed of 60 kmph or less. When the speed of the wind builds up to more than 63 kmph, it becomes a tropical storm. If the speed of the wind increases to 119 kmph, it becomes a hurricane.

Satellite view of a hurricane.

Categories

Hurricanes are put into different categories depending upon the speed with which the wind moves. The highest or first category are reserved for the hurricanes which have a wind speed of 119 to 153 kmph. The fifth and last category is reserved for hurricanes which have a wind speed of 252 kmph.

Categories 1 to 3 of a hurricane can destroy houses.

FUN FACT

A hurricane is named in alphabetical order every year. These names are picked from six lists with 21 names which can be used for six consecutive years. After this, the list is remade.

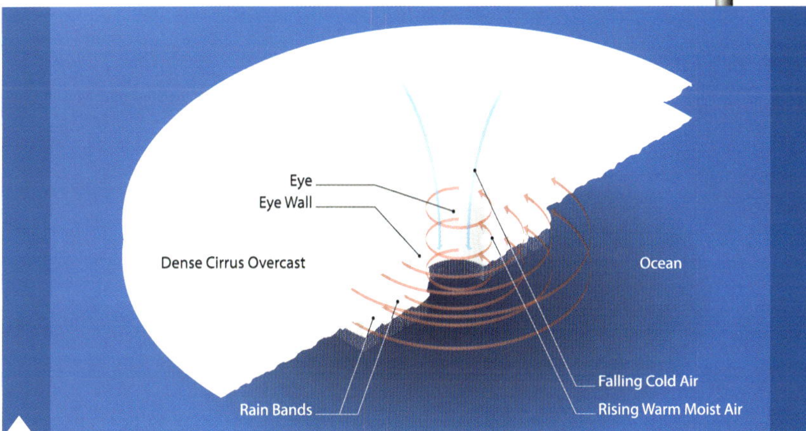

A diagram representing the cross-section of a hurricane.

A satellite grabbing a picture of the hurricane taking place on Earth.

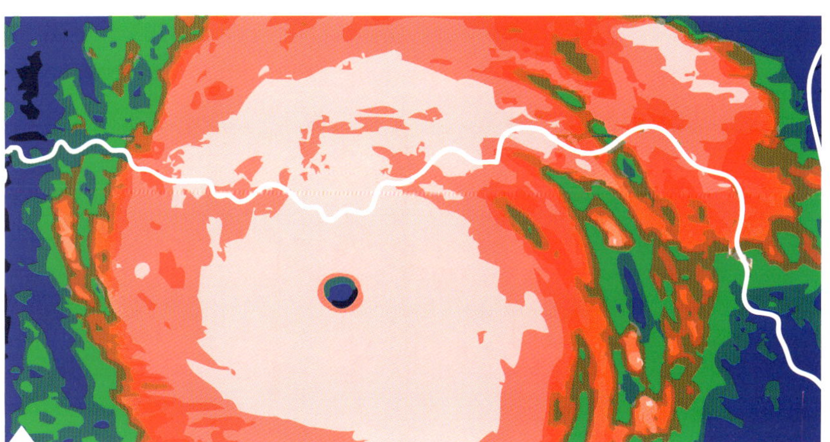

A monitor is used to track the speed and force of the wind and waters.

Parts of a hurricane

A hurricane is also called a typhoon. There are three parts of a hurricane. These are:

- **Eye:** This is a hole at the very centre of the storm. Scientists have managed to capture a picture of this part of the hurricane using special technology. Compared to the rest of the hurricane, this part might seem calm as the clouds are clear or just a little bit cloudy.
- **Eye wall:** This is actually made up of several thunderstorms spinning around the eye. At this point, the storms, winds and rains are the strongest and most severe.
- **Rain bands:** The rain bands are groups of clouds that spread away from the eye wall. Their arrangement largely contributes to the size of the hurricane as they spread far and wide. The rain bands are composed of many hurricanes and a few tornadoes.

How do scientists study hurricanes?

Scientists are able to study hurricanes by various methods. One method is to take a picture. Satellites are able to pick up pictures of hurricanes from space. These pictures are even made public and are displayed on the TV or the internet. There are some instruments which can measure the temperature of the ocean and the clouds above. There are also instruments to measure the speed at which a cloud is moving, the direction in which it is moving, and the height of a cloud.

The data received from these pictures and instruments is put together by scientists to understand the hurricanes. With these methods, scientists have been able to predict hurricanes. This information is released to the public so that they can take measures to protect themselves. It also helps understand how hurricanes are formed and even what can make them grow in strength.

Drought

If a place does not experience rainfall for a long time, and if it does not have other means to supply water to the land, it begins to experience a drought. A drought is an extreme water shortage. The lack of water begins to damage crops and reduces the flow of streams.

Declaring a drought

Usually, if a place has not had rainfall for a long time, people say it is experiencing a drought. But this might not necessarily be the case. The amount of dryness is compared to the average dryness. A drought is declared when the amount of dryness in an area is more than its average for a long period of time. There is no fixed length of time to declare a drought. The time for an arid region is shorter than the time for a place near the coast. Droughts are classified into four types.

Droughts affect an entire region.

Permanent drought

Arid regions and other places with the driest climates experience a permanent drought. East Africa or the Atacama Desert, for example, are places which experience permanent droughts. Drought has affected East Africa since the 1980s to this day. As a result, they need irrigation support to carry out agriculture.

Seasonal and unpredictable drought

Seasonal droughts take place in areas with a rainy and dry climate. The tropical and subtropical climate areas experience seasonal droughts. They have plenty of water during the rainy season, but in the summer and winter, they might experience water shortage and drought. An invisible drought mostly occurs in the summer season due to high evaporation rates. Unpredictable or even regular rainfall cannot heal an invisible drought.

Unpredictable drought

Some areas experience sufficient rainfall. This area might suddenly experience a lack of rainfall or any precipitation. The weather would become hot and the humidity in the air would decrease. Such a drought occurs in humid and sub-humid climate. Unpredictable droughts affect small areas.

Food shortage

Agriculture without any irrigation support becomes difficult during a drought. There is a definite shortage of crops. This creates a shortage of food. Import of crops and other food items might then become a necessity. These things would require lots of money. In poor countries, droughts have resulted in starvation and famines for this reason.

The California droughts dried up the wetlands over a few years.

TSUNAMI

Sometimes, waves as tall as 100 feet come surging from the ocean and crash onto the shore. These waves move faster than a jet plane. With their force and speed, the walls of these waves demolish the structures on the shore within minutes. This series of massive and destructive ocean waves is called tsunami. "Tsunami" is a Japanese word which means "harbour wave".

Causes of a tsunami

The oceanic crust, and the part of Earth below it, undergoes lots of activity. Sometimes, this activity results in an earthquake (on or near the boundaries of tectonic plates), volcanic eruption or a landslide. If a meteor crashes into the ocean, it might also cause a tsunami. As a result, the water above this part of the oceanic crust is displaced (forced into motion) in waves.

On reaching the surface, which has shallow water, the height of these waves increases by a few metres. Their speed is somewhat slowed by the shallow water. As a result, the distance between two consecutive waves reduces, so that they are closer. These waves then reach the ocean with great force.

Approaching tsunami

Tsunamis travel across the ocean at a speed of 800 kmph. This means that they can move across the entire Pacific Ocean in one day. The tall waves gain more and more energy as they move. It is difficult to spot an approaching tsunami. While it approaches, the water at the coast retreats just a little. Then, the tsunami waves hit the shore within the next five minutes. So, retreating coastal water is a major sign of an upcoming tsunami.

Pacific Tsunami Warning System

Early warning of an approaching tsunami is a true blessing as it gives people time to clear the coast and find higher ground. As a result, there are systems built to predict and give early warning of the tsunamis. The Pacific Tsunami Warning System is headed by 26 countries. It is based in Hawaii. It is equipment with technology to measure the seismic waves and find out the water level.

Signs for evacuation during a tsunami.

The growing wave

If seen in the middle of the ocean, a tsunami wave might look only one-foot tall. This is because it is surrounded by deep water. When it reaches the shallow water at the coast, it is at its tallest and more energetic.

Tsunami warning tower.

FLOODS

Floods can occur anywhere on Earth and at anytime. Floods have taken more lives than hurricanes, tsunamis, droughts, volcanic eruptions and earthquakes combined. Compared to other natural disasters, almost all parts of the world experience floods. There are many reasons for floods to take place. It takes lives and destroys property. If an agricultural land is flooded, it causes irrevocable damage to crops.

What is a flood?

Hurricanes, volcanic eruptions or earthquakes which occur in the sea, might displace water to the shore and cause a flood. Or, a dry land might suddenly be swamped with lots of water because of continuous and heavy rainfall or by an explosion of a water reserve. This also causes a flood.

Areas under threat

Floods mostly occur in areas which are close to a water body like a river or ocean. Low-lying areas are often under threat of floods. Seychelles, a group of islands in the Indian Ocean, has a low-lying coast. Giant waves crash against the coast and cause floods.

All rivers can cause floods. The floods that start from big rivers cause more damage as they carry more water, have a wider reach, and also flow with greater speed and force. Mostly, a flood is started by a river when the flow of its water suddenly picks up speed.

Storms and floods

When a storm takes place in a sea, the water is pushed towards the shore. This causes a storm surge, which means that the sea level rises due to the nearing storm. As a result, the shore becomes flooded. If the storm surge takes place at high tide, the flood might even spread beyond the shores. The effects of such floods are deadly. The floods can spread even 1,000 km away from the shore.

Storm waves over a sea.

FUN FACT

When the Mississippi River caused a flood in 1993, it affected an approximately 800 km long and 300 km wide area, destroying over 50,000 homes and damaging crops on almost 20,000 km of farmland.

Floods damage life to a great extent.

The hundred-year flood

A hundred-year flood is a massive, destructive and terrifying flood that takes place once every hundred years. This is not an exact number, it's just a theory. "Hundred years" is used to indicate that there is a one per cent chance that such a flood will occur while storms or heavy rains are building up.

Today, these floods are becoming more and more regular due to changes in the environment. Global warming might be a possible cause. Now, the hundred-year flood has become like a ten-year flood where we might experience a massive flood once every decade.

Duration of a flood

The duration of a flood depends upon how it started. For example, a flash flood lasts for very little time. The waters fill up quickly and also flow out quickly. A flood caused by a storm can take a long time to drain out. It might take days and might need outside intervention. The sea walls built to prevent a flood might actually prevent the water from draining out.

Heavy rainfall and floods

Floods are also caused by heavy rainfall. There are two likely places which are affected by floods for this reason. A river which runs along a low-lying area can cause a highly destructive flood. The extra water from the heavy rainfall rises and increases the speed in which the water flows in the river. This causes an overflow which sends water to the surrounding land, causing a flood.

Some rivers flow along narrow valleys. The water flows with speed in a small area. If the force increases due to heavy rainfall, it can create a moving flood. This is called "flash flood". It moves with great speed, damaging the surrounding valley.

Can you measure rainfall?

Rainfall can be measured using a device called the rain gauge. A rain gauge is used by a meteorologist. It has a funnel which is placed over a small cylinder which is kept inside a bigger cylinder. The rain gauge is kept in a place where rain can fall into the funnel easily. The cylinders have measurements on them. If the inner cylinder fills with water, it flows into the outer cylinder. A meteorologist reads these measurements.

Meteoroidal rain gauges are placed underground.

VOLCANIC ERUPTION

Volcanoes are the cracks or fissures in Earth's crust, out of which molten magma comes out during the eruptions. The volcanoes erupt while the magma is forced to the surface of Earth by the movements of Earth's tectonic plates. Volcanoes are usually in the form of conical mountains, called the volcanic mountains.

What is a volcano?

Volcanoes are the vents on Earth's surface. A volcano is formed when molten rock erupts through the surface of a planet. There is liquid rock inside a volcano called magma. When magma reaches the surface of Earth it flows out through the volcanic vent as lava. Fresh lava ranges from 700° to 1,200 °C. It glows red to white hot as it flows.

What causes a volcanic eruption?

Earth's crust is made up of enormous slabs called plates, which fit together like a pieces of a puzzle. Sometimes, there is movement, causing the plates to move. Between Earth's crust and mantle is a substance called magma, which is made of rock and gases. When two plates collide, one section slides over the other, the one beneath is pushed down. This causes the molten magma (as lava), hot rocks, debris and gases to gush out. This is a volcanic eruption.

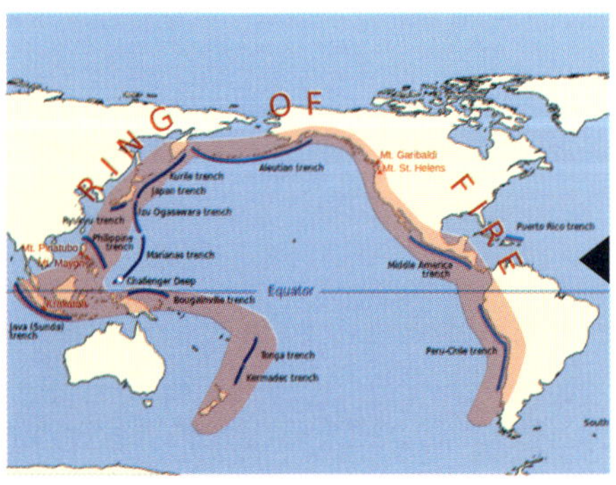

Ring of fire

Most of the islands of Oceania are near the rim of the Pacific tectonic plate. As the plate shifts northwest, it causes significant geological activity, which includes volcanic eruptions. Because of the many active volcanoes along the plate's boundaries, the surrounding shorelines are called the "Ring of Fire".

Volcanic eruption

Volcanoes give out different material, and interestingly each have their own style of erupting. The different types of eruptions result from the differences in magma that each volcano contains. Magma that is low in gas and silica gives out a gentle flow of thin, rapidly spreading lava. In contrast, magma that is rich in gas and silica results in violent explosions. The thick, magma may block the volcanic vent, preventing the upward movement of the magma until the accumulated pressure blows the overlying rock.

Lava flowing into the Pacific Ocean at Big Island, Hawaii.

Arenal Volcano at Costa Rica.

Flows of searing lava can reach upto 1250 °C or more.

Phases of eruption

Geologists classify volcanic eruptions according to four chief forms or phases: Hawaiian, Strombolian, Vulcanian and Peleean.

1. In the **Hawaiian** phase, lava gushes out in a fountain without any volatile eruptions.

2. In the **Strombolian** phase, which gets its name from the Stromboli volcano on an island north of Sicily, thick lava is continuously emitted, but with milder explosions. Lava arcs and steam-driven clouds of ash shower the dome with molten drizzle.

3. A **Vulcanian** phase occurs when magma blocks the volcanic vent. As a result, tons of almost solid magma is thrown into the sky, forming a vapour cloud over the crater.

4. The most violent eruption is the **Peleean**, which gets its name after Mount Pelee on the Caribbean island of Martinique. Fine ash, thick lava and gas-charged clouds are emitted, travelling downhill at a remarkable speed.

FUN FACT

Approximately 91 per cent of the world's earthquakes and 81 per cent of the world's largest earthquakes occur within the Ring of Fire in the Pacific Ocean.

Aftermath of an eruption

Eruptions are often accompanied by severe rains, which then condenses in the atmosphere to form clouds. Explosive gases in the magma, such as hydrogen sulphide, fluorine, carbon dioxide and radon, are let out into the atmosphere upon eruption.

A thick wave of ash, extremely heated gases and rock travels downhill at speeds of more than 100 kmph, filling existing valleys with the fluid mixture. This collapses as it cools and results in a rock formation.

Crater Lake

When a volcano erupts a large volume of material is left unsupported at the centre of the cone. As a result, the crater and walls of the vent collapse into the hollow chamber, creating a large circular depression known as a "caldera" across the summit. The famous Crater Lake in southern Oregon is a result of such an eruption.

TYPES OF VOLCANIC ERUPTIONS

Volcanoes are more often classified according to their status, that is, extinct (unlikely to erupt), dormant (not extinct but temporarily inactive) or active (experiencing frequent eruptions). They can also be classified on the basis of their shape as cinder cone, caldera, composite, shield, submarine or lava dome.

Cinder cone volcanoes

Cinder cone volcanoes are small volcanoes with sharp hills shaped like cones. These hills are made of cinder (from igneous rocks) and ash. The cinder is made up of basalt and andesite. There is very little lava present in its composition. Cinder cone volcanoes are highly explosive. Sometimes, they issue lava.

Because of its shape, a cinder cone volcano is one of the most easily recognisable volcanoes. They have sharp, steep sides and small craters on top. A cinder cone volcano is small, so it can even form of one of the other types of volcanoes.

Cinder cones volcano.

Stratovolcanoes

Stratovolcanoes are also called composite volcanoes. They are made up of lava flows, volcanic ash and cinders. The lava flows are arranged in layers which appear to be in pattern. Volcanic rocks (cinders) and volcanic ash is merged into these flows. They make up some of the most beautiful volcanoes in the world. On an average, a stratovolcano is about 10,000 feet tall.

The slopes of a stratovolcano are quite steep. They contain pyroclastic flows, which is a mixture of dry and hot pieces of rock with hot gases. As these moved from the vent, they caused intense eruptions.

The El Teide volcano in Spain.

FUN FACT

Some volcanoes erupt to take the lives of thousands of people. Other volcanoes destroy entire cities. They are called super volcanoes. Its eruption can be felt all around the planet. The last eruption from a super volcano occurred nearly 75,000 years ago at Toba, Indonesia. There are 40 super volcanoes around the world.

Mauna Loa with visible craters.

Shield volcanoes

Hawaii's erupting Mt Kilauea is a shield volcano. A shield volcano is extremely wide and, like the stratovolcano, it can be as tall as 10,000 feet. It has soft upper slopes which become steep as we go lower from the crater. The lower slopes contain lava. They form from accumulated lava from the central vent which pile up during the eruptions. They have some pyroclastic matter near the vents.

Shield volcanoes form from eruptions which are nonexplosive. These eruptions give out basaltic magma which is not very thick. Shield volcanoes basically make up the islands of Hawaii. Mauna Loa, a shield volcano in Hawaii, rises about 30,000 feet above the ocean floor and is called the largest single mountain in the world. Most shield volcanoes have calderas at the summit.

Diagram of a volcano.

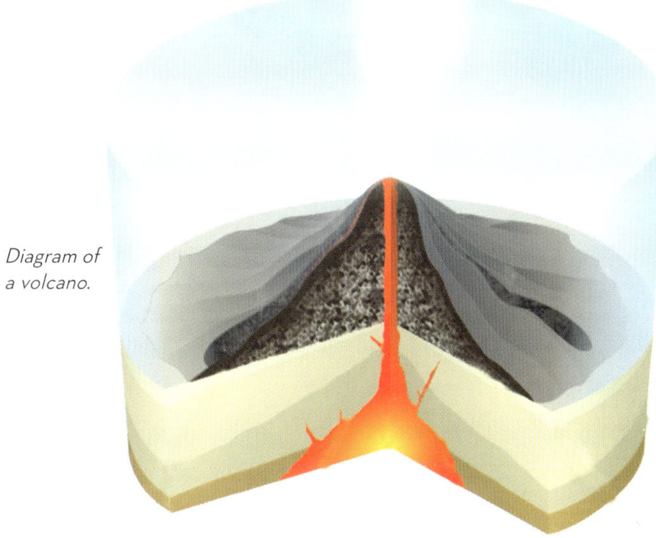

Submarine volcanoes

Submarine volcanoes are cone-shaped. They are mostly found under water. Most submarine volcanoes are active. They erupt under water. Instruments called the hydrophone is used to keep a track of, and detect the eruptions of, the submarine volcanoes around the world.

Lava dome of Paluweh.

Lava domes

Some vents give out thick lava which accumulates in layers without flowing forward. This eventually forms a lava dome. Lava domes have steep mounds which can grow to be around a hundred metres in height. They are wider than they are tall. Lava domes tend to be around 3000 feet wide.

Mt Rinjani with a caldera.

Caldera

If the top of a volcano collapses inwards, it results in the formation of a caldera. It is circular in shape. It might have a small lake present in it. Its edges could have sharp, steep cliffs. Like the cinder cone volcano, it can form on other types of volcanoes.

Calderas are formed when a volcano experiences a massive explosion. A caldera is spotted easily from an aerial view because the change in the structure of the previous volcano is easily spotted. Calderas have a diameter that exceeds a mile.

EARTHQUAKES

Earthquakes occur by the thousands every single day. However, most of them are minor tremors or occur too far beneath Earth's surface and so cannot be felt. Some earthquakes are terribly destructive. They can be felt hundreds of kilometres away. Tall buildings crumble to the ground with every devastating tremor of the earthquake. During an earthquake, the ground begins to shake in several ways.

Fault lines

Earthquakes occur in the areas where two tectonic plates meet. The cracks that mark the merging boundaries of these plates are called "fault lines". These tectonic plates move slowly along. Sometimes, while one plate is moving, the other might move in the opposite direction, or remain in the same position. This causes an earthquake.

During such movement of the plates, a lot of tension builds up in the fault line. This puts a lot of strain on the plates which then force themselves to stand in a new position with a snap. This snap is what creates a shake on Earth's surface.

San Andreas Fault Zone in California, USA.

Hypocentre and epicentre

An earthquake starts right below Earth's surface at a particular point on the fault line. This point is called the "hypocentre" or the "focus". Another point which lies just above the hypocentre is the epicentre. The vibrations experienced during an earthquake begin to build and move along the breaks in the fault line. Earthquakes are classified according to where the hypocentre is located.

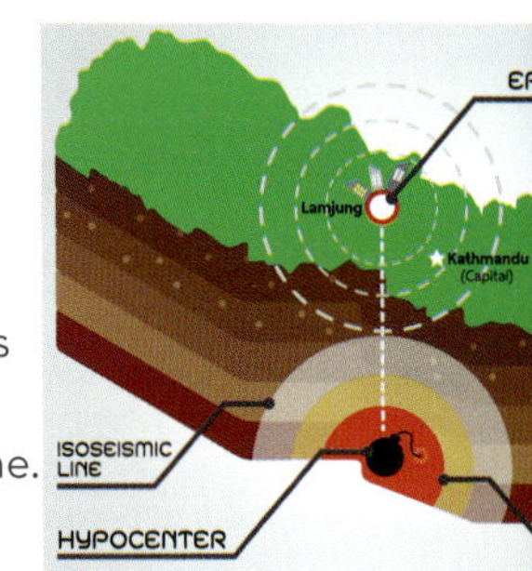

Nepal earthquake.

The Ring of Fire

Most of the earthquakes in our planet take place in and around the Ring of Fire. There is also a lot of volcanic activity that happens here and earthquakes are a result of that. While most earthquakes occur at the fault lines, these earthquakes are hardly noticeable. These earthquakes might not even move a feather on the surface.

It is only when the stress between the plates is released quite suddenly and quickly that the vibrations occur in the area of the fault lines. These vibrations are called seismic waves. They travel thousands of kilometres from their position and reach the surface. Some earthquakes even occur when two plates are squeeze together or stretched apart.

How are earthquakes measured?

Earthquakes are measured in terms of magnitude. Seismologists measure the earthquakes. The vibrations or tremors felt during the earthquakes are recorded and measured using a seismogram. These seismograms create zig-zag lines on paper. The lines made by the seismogram become appear more frantic when the intensity of the tremors increase. Seismologists use the seismogram to understand the epicentre, focal depth and type of fault lines on which the earthquakes took place.

Seismograph instrument

Types of earthquakes

There are two major types of earthquakes. If the hypocentre is at a distance of 0-70 km from the surface, then it is called a shallow-focus earthquake. If the hypocentre is at a distance of 70-700 km from the surface, it is called a deep-focus earthquake.

A shallow-focus earthquake is more powerful, and causes more devastation than a deep-focus earthquake. As they are closer to the surface, the seismic waves reach the surface faster and are stronger when they do. The rocks at the surface apply more strain on the hypocentre.

Types of waves

There are P, S and L waves. They all occur at the time of an earthquake. They move with great energy at first and then lose their energy as they spread. P and S waves travel faster and cover a long distance in a very short time. For example, P and S waves can travel from the South Pole to the North Pole within half an hour. Some obstructions might prevent them from reaching the other end of the world.

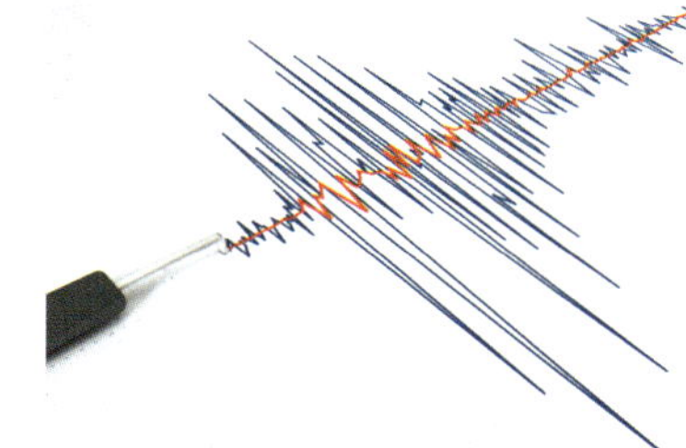

Products of earthquakes

Though earthquakes are destructive, they have helped shape our planet. The islands of Japan, the Himalayas, the state of California and the oil drills are all a product of the earthquakes that have occurred in the past.

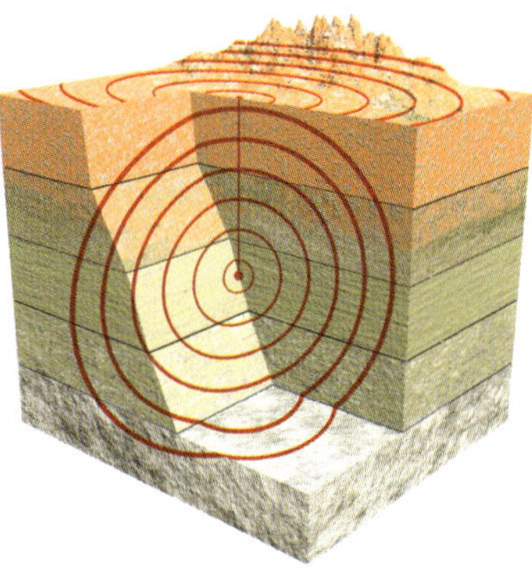

Diagram showing the hypocentre and epicentre of an earthquake.

AVALANCHE

During an avalanche, massive amounts of snow, ice, soil and rocks slide down the slope of a tall mountain with great speed and force. An avalanche can be deathly because the snow sweeps away everything along the way. Landslides are one form of avalanche which push rocks and mud down a slope. However, the most commonly known avalanche is the one where snow slides down with great speed.

Moving downhill

A large chunk of snow becomes unstable and breaks away from its position in the slope. It slides down and gathers speed as it travels down the slope, taking the particles of snow and ice resting on the downhill slope. It moves like a fast-flowing river of ice. The movement also pushes small particles of ice into the air. The avalanche then picks up momentum and speed as it travels downhill.

An oncoming avalanche is captured using special cameras.

Sluff avalanche

During snowfall, layers upon layers of snow pile up on top of one another. This is called a snowpack. There are two types of avalanches that occur as a result of a snowpack. Usually, the topmost layer of a snowpack is weak. There is a lot of sluff on this weak area. A sluff is thin, powdery dry snow which does not have shape. It moves over the snowpack. Sluff avalanches are less destructive than slab avalanches.

Slab avalanche

The weak layer of snow in a snowpack sometimes lies under other layers. The layers above this are crushed and compressed together. The weak layer might break out from below and start an avalanche. The layers on top are then carried along by the weak layer below. This makes the upper, compressed layers slide, tumble and roll down the slope, making the avalanche very unstable.

A slab avalanche carries even large slabs and blocks of ice along. The avalanche makes the blocks break up into several pieces. It creates clouds upon clouds of icy particles which also travel with the avalanche. Slab avalanches are very dangerous. A person can easily get crushed beneath the slab avalanche.

Protection from avalanches

People living near snow-covered mountains protect themselves in several different ways. They build strong, tall fences made of special material to block the oncoming wave of snow. They also build large barriers for the same purpose. Explosives placed at strategic locations get activated when the heavy weight of snow falls upon them. This clears the snow travelling downhill.

An avalanche is similar to a landslide.

WORKING WITH NATURE

Earlier, a majority of the population around the world was involved in farming and agriculture. Civilisations were built close to a source of water so as to grow crops more efficiently. Traditionally, the climate, soil, crops and the relationship between the three were studied in geography.

Later, more branches of geography came about. Those interested in geography can now study one or more of these branches and make a career for themselves. While the traditional occupation of farming still exists, today people can explore careers in the field of climatology, mining, environment management, transportation, communication and city planning. There is a world of opportunities available for all lovers of geography.

DEVELOPING AGRICULTURE

Farming is an ancient occupation. It was undertaken by the people of the Stone Age. The field of agriculture carries a deep respect for nature. Over time, human beings have studied and improved their techniques of farming to produce more and more. No other occupation has affected the landscape of places around Earth like agriculture has.

Beginning of agriculture

Civilisations have been built on the practice of agriculture and farming. Before agriculture, people did not stay in one place. Instead, they travelled in search of animals to hunt. They ate the wild plants which naturally grow on the earth. Thus, the early humans were hunters and gatherers.

Agriculture developed around 12,000 years ago. At that time, people were able to cultivate simple cereal and root crops. The practice of settling down in one place began when people settled next to the crops they had cultivated.

Domestication

Starting from 2000 years ago, agriculture became the main occupation of the world population. Even today, the population of some countries is mostly involved in agriculture or related occupations. Domestication developed alongside. Wild animals were tamed so that they could be used to produce crops. The first wild animal to be tamed were the dogs, and they were used to hunt. Sheep and goat were tamed so that they could supply milk and wool. Cattle like cows and buffaloes were then tamed to work in the farm and to provide milk, butter and cheese.

Cattle used in the farm.

FUN FACT

Early farmers first mastered the technique of growing rice and corn. Research has revealed that farmers in ancient China were growing these crops as far back as 7500 BCE.

Development of agriculture

After domesticating cattle, people developed the techniques of ploughing and pulling. The invention of the wheel helped develop transport. So, people used the available modes of transport to send their crops to different places. Now, people were able to grow more crops than they needed. They used the extra crops to trade for other items. They became involved in selling and trading crops in their free time.

People stayed close to their farms. With this, permanent villages began to develop. The practice of trade drove people to find other villages. Economies now began to develop. The Mesopotamian Civilisation was built along the Nile River in Egypt. It had a successful agricultural community.

Invention of farming tools

Agriculture developed very slowly. With every new invention, its development received a small push. After farmers became acquainted with fire, they used it to control the production of certain wild plants which grew firster when exposed to a wildfire. After axes were developed, they used them to cut down trees and clear out small plots of land on which to farm. They also found methods to store the crops. One example is the clay pots which were used to store and cook food in.

Irrigation

Irrigation systems are said to have developed in the Mesopotamian Civilisation in 550 BCE. Water from the Nile River and some nearby streams was directed to the fields in the inner parts of the civilisation. The entire community came together to build a proper irrigation system which could benefit everybody. This was also seen in the ancient Chinese civilisation. Soon, with improved tools and methods, people were able to grow more variety of crops. They also came up with different food items to make from these crops.

Industrial Revolution and agriculture

The Industrial Revolution took place between the seventeenth and nineteenth centuries. Various machines were invented during this revolution. The machines were used to improve agriculture and the yield of crops. By this period, people were able to grow enough crops for an entire city. Some machines were also used to utilise these crops as raw materials. Cotton came to be used in a machine called the "cotton gin", which produced cotton fibre from seed. Without the machine, the process took a very long time. At the same time, the invention of a thresher shortened the time used to separate grain and seed from chaff and straw.

Cotton field during the time of harvest.

TECHNIQUES IN FARMING

By the 1950s, machines powered by gas and electricity were used in agriculture. Tractors replaced bullocks. Livestock became an important offshoot. Electricity not only provided light on farms but also powered water pumps, livestock feeding machinery and milking machines. With the introduction of pesticides, insecticides and fertilisers, the yield was better. Farmers developed techniques to grow crops and restore the soil.

Permanent crops

Based on the terrain and available resources, farmers pick and choose different techniques of farming to grow their crops. A farmer who has few technological resources available will grow permanent crops. Citrus trees and coffee plants are examples of permanent crops. These do not get replanted with every harvest.

Coffee plant.

Slash and burn

Slash and burn is a technique of farming where land is first cleared with the help of a fire. This fire is controlled and supervised. Before the fire, the farmer cuts up the brush on the plot. This dries the remaining vegetation. Then, the farmer starts a fire which gets rid of the remains of the crops.

The heat from the fire burns the soil and fertilises it. Once the fire is extinguished, the farmer sows seeds of the new crop. When the fertility of soil is exhausted, the farmer moves to a new land. This practice is carried out in temporary farms in Africa and Asia.

Slash and burn is carried out in small areas.

Intercropping

In this technique, crops are planted in rows with large gaps between them. Other crops are planted in these gaps. For example, if a farmer plants kernels of corn in rows, he/she will plant crops of legumes and pulses between the rows. This practice is called intercropping. It reduces soil erosion and prevents loss of moisture in the soil.

Cabbages grown in rows.

Ranching

Ranching is a technique of clearing a land and making it ready for farming. Herds of cows, sheep or buffaloes are let loose on the land. Here, they graze upon the wild plants and grass grown on the land. They also crush some of the bigger plants and shrubs. This creates a grassland. It clears away the grazing animals or predators found her. The animals are controlled by farmers and breeders on horses.

Herds of cows and sheep in the field.

FUN FACT

There are two types of farmers. "Subsistence farmers" grow crops as food for their family. They sell off the surplus crops for money. Commercial farmers grow crops to sell. These crops might also be used as raw materials (cotton for textile industries).

Mixed farming

Mixed farming is the growing of crops and the rearing of livestock on the same farm. Farm animals like sheep are sometimes kept in a field with strong fences. They are not able to wander away from the field. They stay on this field for days. The matter excreted by them is used as fertiliser. The dung and manure which falls on the land fertilises it. Then, the animals are cleared and the field is used for farming.

Before keeping the farm animals in the field, certain crops are grown there. These crops are good for the animals. After the animals are removed, food and cash crops are grown there.

Crop rotation is an important farming technique.

Crop rotation

Crop rotation is one of the most important techniques of farming. It is used by most farmers around the world. A farmer plans which crops to grow in a year (or longer) well in advance. He/she also plans when to grow them. He/she makes a conscious effort to grow different kinds of crops.

Rosemary and beetroot grown by crop rotation.

Benefits of crop rotation

This practice reduces crop diseases. For example, an insect called "rice stem borer" is found in rice farms. If a farmer continues to grow rice on a farm repeatedly, the rice stem borer would multiply and eventually destroy the crops. This is why the rice farmer must grow crop like legumes, beans and bulbs to kill off the insects.

CATCHING FISH

Like agriculture, fishing is one of the oldest occupations in the world. Humans have been fishing for food and trade since ancient times. Mollusks were a part of the diet of the ancient people. The method of using nets and traps to catch fish has been developed by our ancestors. The traps and nets were improved upon with the use of technology.

Classification of fishing

There are several types of equipment used for fishing. This equipment is called "fishing gear". Based on the gear used, fishing is classified into 16 categories like fishing without gear, stunning, line fishing, fishing with lift nets, and harvesting with machines.

Fishing equipment.

Fishing without gear

When fishing without gear, people use small hand tools like knives and hoes. Some people dive into the water (wearing protective suits) and collect fishes, pearls, oysters and corals from the water. Some use hunting animals like otters to fish.

Grappling and wounding gear

While in water, people might use spears or other long-handled tools to catch the fish. Harpoons are one example of long-handled fishing tools. Shellfish are harvested using raking tools. Blowpipes, bows and arrows, and guns and rifles are adapted to work underwater so as to catch bigger fish. Such fishing is carried out in the "grappling and wounding gear" category where fishes are first wounded and then collected.

A fisherman using a spear gun.

Line fishing

Line fishing uses baits and lures to trick fish into coming closer to the device. The bait is artificial. It usually has a hook. The artificial bait is different for different fishes. The hook might be replaced with a gorge if the person using it wants to catch eels. Larger fishes are caught with big hooks which are lowered into the water.

Fishing reel used in the baits of line fishing. .

Boats and nets collected in a fishing harbour in Lebanon.

Fishing harbours

A fishing harbour is highly useful and helpful to all fishermen. It is a safety point for boats. It is at this point that fishermen transfer their morning's catch to the market. It is also a place for the repair, clean up and maintenance of fishing boats and large fishing vessels.

Some fishermen work for certain merchants or fishing industries. They come to the offices of the merchants and industries to unload their day's catch. A fishing harbour is also a place where the fishermen can weigh their catch and decide the pricing. They can also store fishes here.

FUN FACT

In the 1800s, people fished for blubber to make oil for lamps. Because of this, the whale population reduced considerably. By the mid-1900s, the overfishing of cods and herrings almost led to their extinction.

Fishing is also carried out as a recreational sport with a simple fishing rod.

Salmon placed in ice.

Trolling

The trolling method of fishing is used to catch salmon. In this method, one or many fishing lines with attached hooks are drawn in the water behind the vessel. The lines might stay static as the boat moves, or they might sway from side to side. The salmon are caught on these hooks.

Salmon caught with this method are immediately cleaned and then put in ice. They do not have any scars or visible wounds on their bodies. So, troll-caught salmon have a high-market value.

The "otter trawl net".

Trawling

In this method, a cone-shaped net is attached to a trawl vessel. This net is then dragged along the boat in the water. The net allows an opening which catches the fish and traps it in the net. Shrimp, groundfish and scallops are caught using this method of fishing.

Overfishing.

Sustainable fishing

With the improvements in technology, people are able to catch many fishes at once. The problem of overfishing has recently come up, where people are catching fishes at rates which are too high for them to replace themselves.

Overfishing has come back to affect the commercial fishing industry. The yield of fishes has now reduced considerably. People have started to realise that the ocean does not have an infinite number of fish. As a result, the practice of sustainable fishing has come up, where people fish in planned areas only.

EXTRACTING MINERALS

Mining is carried out in all countries and continents except Antarctica. It is the process of extracting minerals from various sources on Earth. These minerals are used as raw materials to produce weapons and tools.

How are mines made?

Mines are created artificially. To create a mine, the land needs to be completely clear of vegetation and animal life. The vegetation is cleared using deforestation techniques like cutting and burning. The bare ground is then drilled and bulldozed. Then, excavators are brought in to extract minerals from the soil on the ground.

Creating mines is damaging the environment.

Products of mining

Minerals occur naturally in nature. Some can be manufactured using lengthy and complex processes. For nearly 1000 years, mining has been carried out to extract gold, silver and copper. Jewellery, ornaments, utensils and coins were made from these minerals. Large ores of minerals were heated to purify them. Iron is one such mineral. It is used as a raw material to make tools. Fuel is made from coal, which is yet another mineral.

There are different techniques of mining, such as surface mining and underground mining. The technique used is dependent upon the mineral to be extracted. Careful research is first carried out on the mining site and then a suitable technique is applied.

An open pit mine.

Miner at work.

The strip mining technique.

Granite carved out of a quarry site.

FUN FACT

Emeralds are mined using gentle techniques. Some part of the mining is done using heavy machinery. Otherwise, groups of people come together and try to mine emeralds using simple tools like shovels.

One of the rarest things is to find a flawless natural emerald. The oldest emerald from South Africa is said to be about 3 billion years old.

Surface mining

Surface mining is used to extract the minerals that lie close to Earth's surface. More than 60 per cent of the total yearly supply of minerals in the world comes from surface mining techniques. There are three types of surface mining techniques:

Open-pit mining: A pit is dug in the area where the minerals are present. If the purpose is to build a large pit, then the pit will have a depth of about 40-50 feet and a width of about 65-100 feet. The minerals are then extracted from the mine created.

Strip mining: In this technique, unwanted rocks and soils are cleared from the layer of minerals lying beneath. The exposed mineral is then extracted.

Quarrying: This technique is mainly used to extract stone, which can be used in the construction of buildings and sculptures. Stone is valuable for its aesthetic appeal. To extract stone, a mine is first created by explosion or with machinery. Then, stone is quarried from the mine.

Hydraulic mining

Some structures are made up of softer rocks and sediments. If there are heavy metals like gold present in these sediments, they can be extracted using a technique called "hydraulic mining". In this method, a high-pressure hose is used to wash down the sediments. The waste from the sediments flows away with the water. The metal remains. This metal can then be used as raw material. However, this method causes pollution of the nearby rivers and brings forward the process of erosion.

Gravel pit

Gravel is mined from pits that are dug out with the help of machinery. Sand is another valuable mineral dug out in this way. Gravel and sand together are used in large quantities around the world, all year round, in the construction industry. Gravel is extracted from the sea bed using dredgers. Pure sand is used to make glass. Finer forms of gravel is used to make clay.

Mass Production

Industries changed the way of living within a few years. Before industries came into the picture, people were mainly into agriculture and animal husbandry. They lived in villages and towns. After industries began to develop, people moved to the cities and started working in factories. They made more money and were able to afford more things. They worked for shorter hours and were able to indulge in hobbies. Industries changed the lifestyle of people around the world.

What are industries?

Industries are a group of organisations that might be involved in either making or supplying goods and services to the masses. Some industries might be involved in both. Based on their size and the work they do, industries are classified as primary, secondary and tertiary industries.

Supply material in an industry.

Primary industries

Primary industries supply raw materials. The fishing industry is a primary industry as it supplies fishes and other aquatic animals. These raw materials are then sold to the food and medicine industries. Primary industries are dominant in developing and underdeveloped countries. In this countries. Agriculture, forestry, fishing and mining are examples of primary industries.

Fishing industry.

Secondary industries

Secondary industries manufacture products from the raw materials supplied by primary industries. In this industry, raw materials are processed and consumer goods are prepared. Some secondary industries also produce energy, like hydroelectricity and fuel. The construction industry is a part of the secondary industry.

Construction industry.

Types of primary industries

Raw materials can be renewable or non-renewable. The extractive industry is a branch of the primary industry. In such industries, people supply raw materials that are non-renewable, such as coal. In the genetic industry, people supply raw materials which can be produced at a faster rate through human intervention. The agriculture industry is an example of the genetic industry.

Tertiary industries

Tertiary industries provide services. They do not produce goods or raw materials like the other two industries. These industries also manage and generate wealth. The retail, banking and investment, finance, investment and transport industries are a part of this industry type.

Transportation as tertiary industry.

Consumer goods

The primary and secondary industries produce goods. The secondary industry mainly produces consumer goods. These goods are purchased by consumers or buyers to satisfy their needs or wants. The buyers could be anyone from the common man to other industries. There are three types of goods—durable, nondurable and services. Services refers to nontangible goods produced by the tertiary industry.

FUN FACT

Industries, factories and the manufacturing processes all simultaneously developed during the industrial revolution. This revolution started in 1760.

Durable goods

Durable consumer goods are those which last for three or more years. Computers and laptops are examples of durable goods. Depending on the type, some amount of maintenance might be required on these goods. This brings in maintenance services. As they last for a longer period of time, durable goods are sometimes priced quite high. Affording these goods is sometimes a luxury.

Nondurable goods

These goods are purchased for immediate consumption. Food items like fruits and pastries are examples of nondurable goods. The clothing industry also produces nondurable goods. Nondurable goods last for three years or less.

Capital goods

Capital goods are a type of durable goods. Buildings, apartments and machinery are examples of capital goods. Maintenance services created for the care and maintenance capital and durable goods. If the citizens of a country buy many durable goods, then the maintenance services will also be in demand. Thus, in many countries, a successful secondary industry gives rise to a successful tertiary industry.

Nondurable goods.

MOVING AROUND THE WORLD

Transportation is a type of industry. It connects the citizens of the world. Transport and industry have changed the lifestyle of human beings. When European explorers travelled to Africa and Asia, they were exposed to new cultures, beliefs, religions and goods. They borrowed some of their culture and traded lots of their goods.

Public transport

Public transport is a service and is a part of the tertiary industry. The governments of all countries offer public transport to their citizens. This enables the citizens to move around the country. The major means of public transport are trains, buses, aeroplanes and ferries.

Benefits of public transport

Public transport is much cheaper than private transport, as not everybody in a city or town can afford to buy a car. Too many cars on the road cause heavy traffic jams. Moving from one part of the city or town to another would become slow and troublesome. If more time is spent in moving from one place to another, then less work would be done. This affects the economy. It also causes heavy pollution. Public transport reduces the number of cars on the road, thus reducing pollution.

Metro trains are seen in developed cities. They can transport thousands of people at one time.

Transporting goods

Railways have grown in importance since the mid-nineteenth century. They developed with the industrial revolution. They do not only transport people but also goods. Goods trains are seen in many countries. They are used to transport different kinds of goods to all parts of the country. Building railway tracks is very expensive and it disrupts nature. However, railway transport is one of the cheapest and most efficient means of transport. It uses less energy.

FUN FACT

Some countries use trolleybuses which run on electricity. These buses move on tracks built on the roads. Above the tracks there are wires which the buses are connected to.

Buses

Buses are big vehicles that can easily carry around 25-50 people, depending on their size. Most countries have a planned bus transport system. Buses start at one point called "stop". Each bus is assigned one route, which it takes daily. The buses drop and pick up passengers at many stops before reaching their destination. Like cars, buses run on gasoline or petrol. Some even run on environmentally friendly fuel like natural gas.

Highways

A highway is a main road which connects long distances like two cities or towns. Most developing countries, and all developed countries, have large highway networks. Highways reduce traffic jams and congestion. It also reduces the time of transport.

Ships and ferries

Shipping as a means of transport has been around for many centuries. Early explorers travelled to different parts of the world by ships. Today, ships are not much used to transport people. Instead, they have become a cheap and efficient way of transporting goods. Some large ships are used as cruises.

Ferries are smaller boats. They transport goods locally. They also transport people to short distances. Land transport might be difficult, time-consuming, expensive or exhausting in places that neighbour bodies of water. Ferries provide a cheaper and faster alternative. Ferries run on fossil fuels.

Air transport

Air transport is an expensive but speedy means of transport. Traditionally, air transport was used to transport people from one country to another. Today, many countries provide air transportation to people wanting to travel from one part of the country to another.

Aeroplanes, helicopters and jets are the modes of air transport. They pick up and drop people from an airport. The construction of an airport is expensive. It takes up a lot of resources. It also changes the landscape of the surrounding area.

Infrastructure

A country's infrastructure is made up of its transportation systems, communication systems, power supply channels, water supplies and drainage systems. The infrastructure in developed countries is mostly well-maintained.

CONSERVING THE ENVIRONMENT

Progress in industry and transport has created problems like pollution and global warming. The population of the world has been increasing at alarming rates in the past century. There are about 7 billion people in the world today and this number is only growing. More and more resources are being demanded every day. This is why it is important to conserve the environment.

Pollution from industries

There are many factories and industries that produce lots of raw materials and goods on a daily basis. They require lots of energy and electricity. They produce billion tonnes of waste. They pollute water sources with waste. It is important for factories and industries to have regular checks and curb their waste production. Left unchecked, they are potential threats to the environment.

Factories release lots of harmful gases into the environment.

Waste

The production of waste has greatly increased since the mid-twentieth century. USA produces nearly 220 million tonnes of waste every year. Only a portion of this waste is reusable. Most countries are facing a problem where the unusable waste is piling up in a pit.

Metal, plastic, paper and glass are reusable wastes.

Environmental conservation

"Environmental conservation" refers to the upkeep and maintenance of the environment. It also means to rebuild and save the environment. Human beings rely on plants for oxygen and food. There are fewer diseases in natural environments than in congested and polluted environments. Human beings also need animals. Otherwise, the circle of life will be disrupted. Hence, environmental conservation refers to taking sensible steps to save the environment from pollution and damage.

Preventing waste

Renewable resources are wasted when we produce items that are simply thrown away. It is our responsibility as citizens of the world to make sure that resources (especially non-renewable resources), go into creating useful and valuable things. Also, that the goods and materials purchased are not wasted. It is also the responsibility of the world citizens to ensure that all forms of energy are used wisely.